Editor

Mary S. Jones, M.A.

Managing Editor

Ina Massler Levin, M.A.

Illustrator

Kelly McMahon

Cover Artist

Tony Carrillo

Art Production Manager

Kevin Barnes

Art Coordinator

Renée Christine Yates

Imaging

Craig Gunnell

Publisher

Mary D. Smith, M.S. Ed.

Grades 1–2

LESSONS USING LEARNING BAGS

for

WRITING

Includes activities for:
- Poetry
- Story Elements
- Story Writing
- Visual Presentation

Designed to meet Writing Standards

Author

Diane L. Nees

Teacher Created Resources

Teacher Created Resources, Inc.

6421 Industry Way

Westminster, CA 92683

www.teachercreated.com

ISBN-1-4206-3187-X

©*2006 Teacher Created Resources, Inc.*

Made in U.S.A.

Table of Contents

Introduction

Gift bags are amazing! Their purpose is to contain and transport needed materials. In this case, when used in the classroom, these same bags can contain and transport an incredible number of skills and strategies to students. Gift bags are so colorful, plentiful, easy to use, and inexpensive. What more could a teacher want?

Everywhere you look there are gift bags with designs that fit into any curriculum. Bags come in a multitude of sizes and shapes, which makes coordinating them with lessons, stories, or units a fairly simple task. Make this your goal. Keep a watchful eye out for bag designs that fit your stories or curriculum. In this book, "small" refers to a 7" x 9" bag, "medium" refers to 10" x 12", and "large" refers to 12" x 14". These are approximate sizes and can certainly vary some, depending on the room you have or the bag you find. For many of the activities, the bags are the transport—that is, they will hold all the other materials needed, thereby keeping everything in one spot and readily accessible. All you need to do is copy the "Bag Tag" and use wide, clear tape to attach it to the gift bag as a label for that activity. The color and/or design of each gift bag is up to you. The more colorful and attractive the design of the bags, the more students will inquire about its contents. It is recommended that the bags you choose have sturdy handles.

Bags are versatile and store easily. They can fold flat to fit inside of a file. Bags can also collapse so you can fit several in a plastic basket to take out and fill as needed. In addition, they can be held on hooks on your bulletin board or around the room. An added bonus is that their designs will add to your classroom décor.

Bags have a great attribute of space . . . unknown space. Students are naturally intrigued by such space and will want to fill that space or find out what's in it. That is the key . . . to motivate! When students are intrigued and motivated—and they will be—you'll open the door to opportunities; active learning experiences; and knowledge of strategies that will promote, challenge, and increase students' understanding. With this understanding, they will learn to become life-long learners.

The activities within these pages meet the McREL writing standards, which are listed below. All standards are used with permission from McREL.

- Uses the general skills and strategies of the writing process.

- Uses grammatical and mechanical conventions in written compositions.

- Uses listening and speaking skills for a variety of purposes.

Copyright 2004 McREL

Mid-continent Research for Education and Learning

2550 S. Parker Road, Suite 500

Aurora, CO 80014

Telephone: (303) 337-0990

Website: www.mcrel.org/standards-benchmarks

Add-On Stories

Motivation is the key to successful student writing. Anyone will put forth his or her most creative effort in writing when someone has really tuned in to what makes them spark. This gives them reason to feel proud of what they do. This learning bag is sure to motivate and inspire!

Materials and Preparation

- ✏ 1 medium gift bag, labeled Add-On Stories
- ✏ 1 copy of Title Sheet, page 5
- ✏ 1 copy of Add-On Forms for every two students (teacher will also need a copy) cut apart, page 6

Procedure

1. After a discussion with students about story topics, vote on a fiction or non-fiction topic that the class would like to write about. Explain to students that the entire class will write one story, with each student writing a small part. This will take many days, as students cannot write their portions until the previous student has finished.

2. Complete the Title Sheet with the story information, and place it in the corner of an empty bulletin board so that student writings can be added in order. Copy the Add-On Forms and cut the pages apart. Number each form up to one more than the number of students in your class, and place all copies in the gift bag. Hang the gift bag so it is easily accessible to students.

3. You start with Add-On Form #1. Keeping with the chosen topic, start the class story with two to three sentences. Explain to students that you will decide the order in which they will write. When it is a student's turn, he or she will go to the gift bag and take the next number form. Each student is expected to write one or two sentences following the sequence and the logic of the story. Add each completed form to the bulletin board.

4. Each day, read all completed forms in order. Students should remember the contents and flow of the story. Discuss possible events and ideas that future students can write about.

5. Read the final (completed) story aloud to students. You may choose to rewrite or type the entire story onto one piece of paper and make a copy for each student to keep. Repeat this procedure, choosing a different topic each time.

Bag Tag

Add-On Stories

Title Sheet

Our Add-On Story
is called

_____

_____

It is all about

_____

_____

Add-On Forms

Add-On Form # _____

_____

_____

_____

_____

By: _____

Add-On Form # _____

_____

_____

_____

_____

By: _____

Alphabet Stories

Alphabet stories are good tools for helping young students learn about paragraphs. With practice, they will soon become proficient in identifying paragraph forms, indenting, beginning each paragraph with a different word, and realizing that each paragraph must to speak to one topic.

Materials and Preparation

- 1 medium gift bag, labeled My Alphabet Story

- several copies of each Alphabet Story Form, pages 8–10

- 1 paper lunch bag for each student, label each bag My Alphabet Story

- scraps of varying colors of construction paper

- scissors

- glue

Procedure

1. Lead an oral discussion with the class about writing sentences, paragraphs, and topics. Explain to students that they will each write a three-paragraph story using one of the Alphabet Story Forms.

2. Have students choose one of the story forms. They should write three short paragraphs for their story topic—two to three sentences each. Students need to begin each paragraph using a word with the assigned letter.

3. Once checked, give each student a paper lunch bag and have him or her place the completed form inside of the bag.

4. Next, each student will make one 3-D item related to something specific in the story he or she wrote, using construction paper, scissors, and glue.

5. Once all students have finished writing their stories and making a related item, it's now time to share! Have student volunteers share their stories and their created objects.

Bag Tag

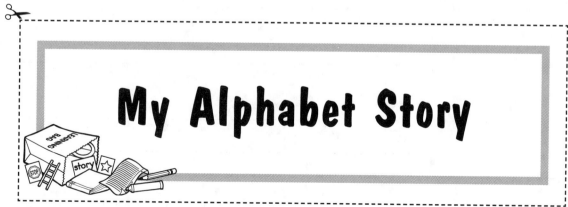

My Alphabet Story

Alphabet Story Form 1

Title _____

A _____

_____

_____

_____.

C _____

_____

_____

_____

_____.

D _____

_____

_____

_____.

Alphabet Story Form 2

Title _____

F _____

_____

_____

_____.

G _____

_____

_____

_____

_____.

M _____

_____

_____

_____.

Alphabet Story Form 3

Title _____

N _____

_____

_____

_____.

S _____

_____

_____

_____.

T _____

_____

_____

_____.

Around the Clock

Sequencing, especially in writing and story telling, presents organizational problems to young writers. Their ideas may be formulated in their minds very nicely, but to get across the sequence of events in written form can be quite difficult. A clock, in this bag activity, will help students express the abstract in concrete terms.

Materials and Preparation

✏ 1 Around the Clock Planner per student, page 12

✏ 1 paper grocery bag per student

✏ 6 small index cards per student

✏ 1 brad per student

✏ tape

Procedure

1. Start by discussing time and events. Students' first time at this should relate to themselves.

2. Have students recall and discuss what they do on an ordinary day in their lives, beginning at six o'clock in the morning.

3. Distribute an Around the Clock Planner to each student. On the planner, students will write a few words about what they do during that time of day in the outside circle. They should draw pictures that relate to what they do on the inside circle.

4. Next, attach the planner at the center to the front of the paper grocery bag with a brad. The planner sheet should be able to spin.

5. Referring to their planners, students should write complete sentences for each time frame on an index card.

6. Then, students can use the index cards as they type their stories, in sequence, on computers (if available) and print. Store the completed stories in the bag, or affix it to the outside, opposite their planner. Index cards should be kept inside. Students can see the progression of time and writing by looking at all parts of the bag.

7. As they write these stories, they can move to any topic and replace times with time words such as: *first*, *next*, *then*, and *finally*.

Around the Clock Planner

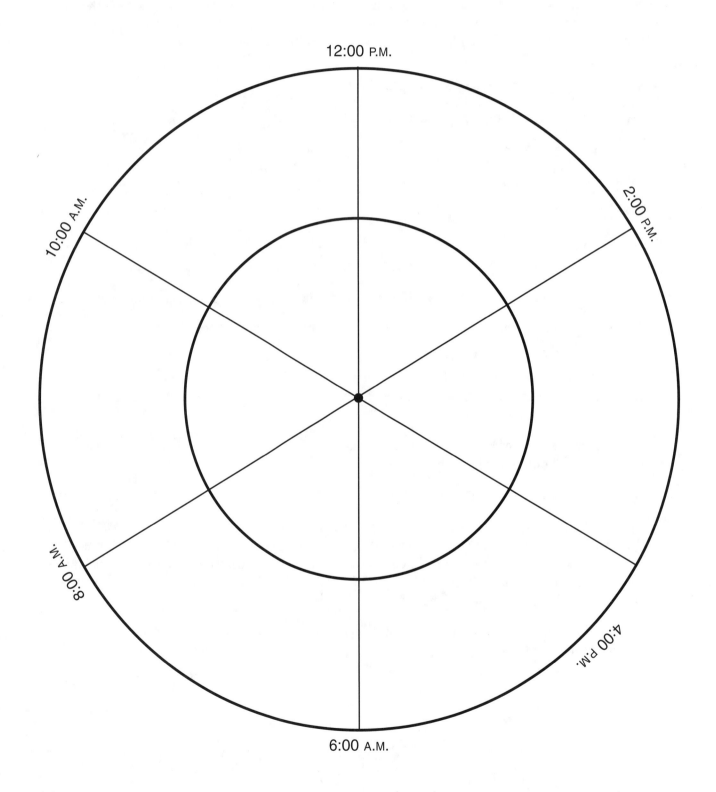

12:00 P.M.

2:00 P.M.

4:00 P.M.

6:00 A.M.

8:00 A.M.

10:00 A.M.

12

Brick Story Building

Bricks and mortar can be great visuals for helping young writers learn how story elements build to make a story stronger. In this teaching bag, you will carry the visuals and the planners for your students to learn to make a strong plan, and thus be able to write a good story.

Materials and Preparation

- 1 medium gift bag, labeled Brick Story Building
- 1 copy of Brick Story Building Planner per student, page 14
- 4 fake cardboard bricks, one of each labeled Characters, Setting, Problem, and Solution
- strips of gray construction paper for mortar

Procedure

1. Help start the writing thought process by laying the "bricks" on a white board or easel. Leave off the "mortar" for now. At the same time, make an analogy between a story with strong writing and one that falls apart. Explain that "mortar words" (details) can be adjectives or any descriptive words that hold the main elements together.

2. Discuss the story elements: characters, setting, problem, and solution. Read a story that is familiar to the students and have them identify the different elements in that story. Write their responses in the different bricks. Discuss how details help tie things together to build a story. Ask for details of the story you read, and write down the students' responses on the gray construction paper strips.

3. Distribute the Brick Story Building Planner to students and have them plan the elements of a story they would like to write. Remind them to start at the bottom of the page.

4. As students finish, go over the planner with them individually, having them verbally tell their story to you.

5. They may retell the story to the class, or if you feel they are ready, have them begin their first written draft.

Sample Brick Story Building using *Where the Wild Things Are* by Maurice Sendak:

Solution: Max decides to go home	
Mortar Words (Details): when Max gets home, his dinner is waiting for him	
Problem: Max gets punished for being a wild thing and leaves to a land across the ocean	
Mortar Words (Details): Max becomes king of the wild things	
Characters: Max, wild things	**Setting:** bedroom, forest where the wild things are
Mortar Words (Details): boy, monsters with big teeth and yellow eyes	**Mortar Words (Details):** lots of trees, next to an ocean

Bag Tag ✂

Brick Story Building

Brick Story Building Planner

Remember, a story always starts with a good foundation. Make sure to start your story at the bottom of this page.

Solution:

Mortar Words (Details):

Problem:

Mortar Words (Details):

Characters: Setting:

Mortar Words (Details):   Mortar Words (Details):

Feely Boxes

Students will love the feely boxes. They provide an excellent tactile method for helping students to elicit and recall adjectives, which they will need for any writing project. Use these boxes as a pre-writing activity and you'll be amazed at the response you get in terms of students transferring the use of adjectives to their writing.

Materials and Preparation

- ✏ 1 medium gift bag, labeled Feely Boxes (Bag Tag on page 16)
- ✏ 2 or more Feely Boxes (see assembly instructions below)
- ✏ 1 copy of Touch and Feel for each student, page 17
- ✏ 1 copy of My Feely Trip for each student, page 18

Feely Box Assembly Instructions

For each box you will need:

- 1 cardboard box (large enough for students to reach their arms into)
- About 20 items of different textures to put inside. Examples include: pencil, eraser tip, stone, shell, pom-pom, button, small stuffed animal, wadded up piece of tin foil, marble, small rubber ball, rubber band, paper clip, pinecone, acorn, pack of unopened gum, small plastic cup, plastic spoon, magnet, quarter, cotton balls, sand paper, etc.
- duct tape
- piece of felt material (optional)

1. Place all items inside the cardboard box.
2. Duct tape the box shut.
3. Cut a hole just large enough for students' arms to go through. Be sure not to make the hole too big.
4. Optional: Tape a piece of felt over the hole in the box and cut a slit through it. This way, students' arms can still go through the hole, while making it hard for them to peek through.

Feely Boxes *(cont.)*

Procedure

1. Begin by explaining to students that good writers use lots of adjectives in their writing. As a whole group, define what adjectives are, and then brainstorm and list several adjectives.

2. Distribute the copies of Touch and Feel to students, and place the students into groups, depending on the number of Feely Boxes you make.

3. Have students take turns feeling for objects in the boxes and describing them. Remind students that they cannot look through the hole of the box. As students feel the objects, they should write down (on the Touch and Feel Form) the adjectives that come to mind to describe the objects. For example, if they feel a cotton ball, they may write the word *soft*.

4. After students complete the Touch and Feel form, they will have a working list of adjectives to use for any story writing, as well as with the My Feely Trip form.

5. Distribute the copies of My Feely Trip to students. Explain that they need to fill in the blanks of the story with words, most being adjectives. They should use the adjectives from the Touch and Feel form for reference. After all students have completed the stories, ask for volunteers to share their stories. You're sure to get some laughter out of the students!

Bag Tag

Touch and Feel

I feel something:

1._____

2. _____

3. _____

4. _____

5. _____

6. _____

7. _____

8. _____

9. _____

10. _____

11._____

12._____

My Feely Trip

I went on a trip through an unknown tunnel. My hand touched

something _____ and _____.

I thought it must be a _____

_____. I twisted my hand around a huge

_____ that felt _____ and

_____. At least I think that's what it was! All of a

sudden I felt a small _____ and

_____ thing that I figured must have been a

_____.

   I couldn't stop from touching! I had to feel the rest of the

_____ things. They were _____

to my touch. I was sure that if I kept digging, I just might find a

_____ ! I'm glad I didn't!

Fusion Stories

A "fusion story" allows writers to use a variety of people, places, and things to create one complete thought. Fusion stories begin with a pick of the cards! Students will choose from three sets of cards and their choices will serve as a "seed" idea for writing. They will need to blend their cards together creatively to make a story with a good beginning, middle, and end.

Materials and Preparation

- 1 small gift bag, labeled Fusion Stories
- 1 set of Who Cards, page 20, cut apart and glued onto red construction paper, then laminated (if possible) and cut apart again so that there is a red border around each one
- 1 set of What Cards, page 21, cut apart and glued onto yellow construction paper, then laminated (if possible) and cut apart again so that there is a yellow border around each one
- 1 set of Where Cards, page 22, cut apart and glued onto blue construction paper, then laminated (if possible) and cut apart again so that there is a blue border around each one
- 3 resealable plastic bags to store each set of cards
- lined writing paper for each student

Procedure

1. Discuss with students how writers get ideas for story writing. Try to keep it in a three part formula, i.e. "Who?", "Does what?", and "Where?"

2. Practice some ideas orally by brainstorming. Encourage students to think of fantasy topics that are unrealistic as well.

3. Take the Who Cards, What Cards, and Where Cards out of the gift bag. Explain to students that separating the story elements is another way to get story ideas. By selecting a card from each category, a new story idea will be created each time. Without looking, draw a card from each of the bags, and model how this idea is like a story seed—it can make ideas grow! Model beginning, middle, and end as each applies to the level of your students.

4. Students should take turns picking three cards to create a unique story idea, one from each bag, and lay them on their desktops. For example, the Who Card could be "A dog," the What Card could be "cries all day," and the Where Card could be "at the movies." The final story idea would be, "A dog cries all day at the movies."

5. Have students write a first draft of their stories, which you can edit. After they rewrite, have them share their completed stories. Sometimes, the more unrealistic the story the more interesting it is!

Bag Tag ✂

Fusion Stories

Who Cards

A dog	The new girl
One green frog	A magic duck
A young boy	A teacher
Two fine ladies	A pro ball player
My special cat	My silly aunt
An older brother	A sleepy bird
The tiny alien	A baby
Bixby, the puppy,	A happy king
An old man	The giant
My best friend	A talking shoe

What Cards

gets wet	drops the books
falls on a log	laughs at jokes
buys two cones	plants a garden
speeds away	feeds the animals
eats everything	washes six cars
hurts one leg	walks in puddles
sleeps for hours	sells hot dogs
races a bike	waters plants
cries all day	finds ten shells
hunts for fish	jumps up and down

Where Cards

at the beach.	in the big house.
in the classroom.	around the block.
at the store.	in a castle.
on the floor.	at the table.
at the circus.	in the park.
in a pond.	at the movies.
under an umbrella.	in a restaurant.
at a factory.	near the zoo.
in the field.	by the woods.
under the bed.	inside the barn.

     22

Ladder Writing

Many students tend to write very short sentences. Even at a young age, students should be taught to put thought into a sentence, and make it interesting and longer than a couple of words. When frequently practiced, writing becomes a habit. Students need to have a strategy to achieve the goal of developing a good habit.

Materials and Preparation

- ✎ 1 medium gift bag, labeled Ladder Writing
- ✎ 2 magnet strips (24" x 2") to construct ladder sides
- ✎ 8 magnet pieces
  - • 5 need to be 4" x 2" for rungs, labeled with Rung Tags, page 24
  - • 3 need to be 3" x 2" for helpers between the ladder rungs, labeled with Helper Tags, page 24
- ✎ several copies of Ladder Writing Form, page 25

Procedure

1. Using a magnetic surface (chalkboard or whiteboard), model "ladder writing" according to the Ladder Writing Form. Use the magnetic pieces to allow students to see the sentence build up. Explain to students that the structure of the ladder will help them write a story.

2. When you put the "Who?" rung up, ask students for an idea of who the story could be about. Choose one of their responses to write at the right of the ladder. For example, "A boy." Write the number of words (2) to the left of the ladder. Next, put up the Adjective Helper Tag, ask for them to describe the boy, then choose a response to write at the right of the ladder. For example, "A smart boy." Now write the number of words (3) to the left of the ladder. Continue this procedure until you have gone through the entire set of magnetic pieces. You will have built your ladder (from the bottom up) and written a complete sentence. An example of a final complete sentence could be, "A <u>smart</u> <u>boy</u> <u>ran</u> <u>quickly</u> <u>to the policeman</u> <u>to get help</u>." (Number of words = 11)

3. Distribute a copy of the Ladder Writing Form to each student. They are ready to make sentences. Stress that they must start at the bottom of the ladder, keep the same words, and add more words as they go up the ladder.

4. Share the complete sentences when students finish. Practice this activity several times so that students can get in the habit of writing long, complete sentences.

Bag Tag

Rung and Helper Tags

Rung Tags: Laminate (if possible), cut out, and glue onto magnetic rung pieces.

Who?

Did what?

How?

Where?

Why

Helper Tags: Laminate (if possible), cut out, and glue onto magnetic helper pieces.

Adjective

Connector Word (so, and, or, because)

Adverb

Ladder Writing Form

**Number
of Words**

_____

_____

_____

_____

_____

_____

| Why? |
| Connector Word (so, and, or, because) |
| Where? |
| How? |
| Adverb |
| Did what? |
| Adjective |
| Who? |

A _____ _____ _____

_____ _____

_____ .

A _____ _____ _____

_____ _____ .

A _____ _____ _____

_____ .

A _____ _____ _____ .

A _____ _____ .

A _____ .

Movie Reels

This bag activity offers a fun way to motivate and display student writing! Students love to pretend, and here's their chance. Whether they've written an original story or retold one, they can share it by reeling their film!

Materials and Preparation

- ✏ 1 large gift bag, labeled Movie Reels
- ✏ 1 reel for the class or 1 reel per student using Movie Reel Frame, page 27 (see instructions below)
- ✏ 2–3 Movie Reel Writing Forms per student, page 28
- ✏ scissors
- ✏ crayons
- ✏ tape

To Make Reels:

- Copy Movie Reel Frame (page 27) and cut it out along the outer edge. Then, cut out the white center along the dashed lines.
- Cut out a piece of tag board the same size as the Movie Reel Frame.
- Laminate the Movie Reel Frame and cut off any lamination on the outside of the frame. Tape the long sides of the frame to the same size piece of tag board.
- The top and bottom are open so students can slide their writing through the center. It will show through the lamination.

Procedure

1. After students have written a story, have them transfer their stories onto the Movie Reel Writing Forms. They can then draw pictures in the rectangles to illustrate the text on each form.
2. If you choose to use the assembled laminated reels, have students cut out their writing along the dashed lines then tape all completed forms together in story sequence.
3. Place the connected forms through the top or bottom of one of the reels. Students can share their stories by pulling their forms through the reels, revealing the words and pictures through the lamination. Have students use their reels frequently to retell a story or to write an original.
4. If you choose not to use the assembled laminated reels, cut out the completed Movie Reel Writing Forms (including the frame) and tape them together so that each page of writing has a frame. Students can then share their stories. You can display the completed Movie Reel stories on a bulletin board.

Bag Tag

Movie Reel Frame

Movie Reel Writing Form

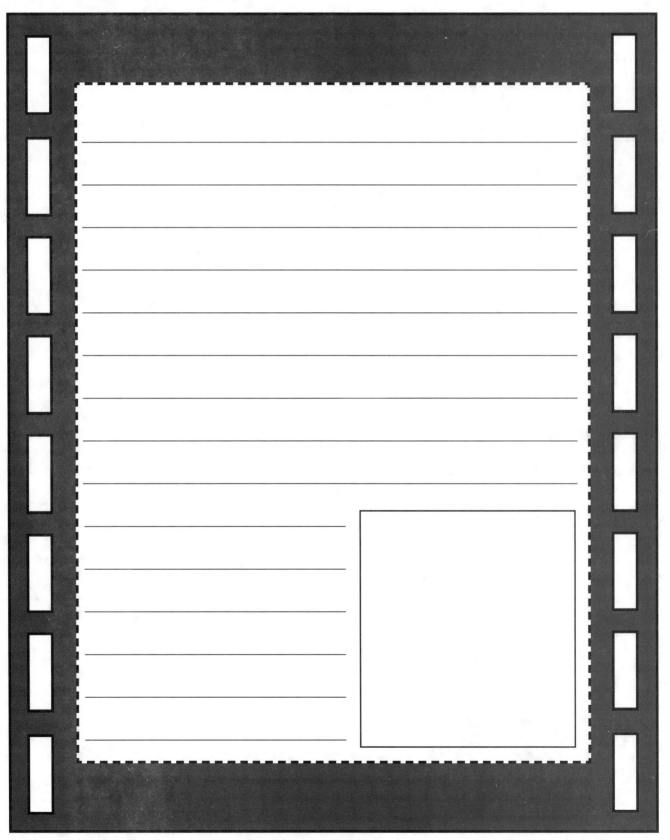

Paragraph Forms

Students need structure when writing a paragraph. Even academically advanced students benefit from having guidelines that spell out exactly what is needed. They should walk through this thought process several times before writing paragraphs independently.

Materials and Preparation

- ✏ 1 medium gift bag, labeled Paragraph Forms
- ✏ 1 copy of the three paragraph writing steps for each student stapled together, pages 30–32
- ✏ 1 large manila envelope filled with old calendar pictures that would help elicit good story ideas

Procedure

1. Remove the envelope of calendar pictures from the gift bag. Lay them out and discuss story possibilities with students. Be specific. For example, hold up a picture of a cake, and suggest writing about a birthday party. Hold up a picture of a dog, and suggest writing about caring for a pet.

2. Have each student choose a picture that gives him or her ideas. Each student should place his or her selection on the corner of his or her desk.

3. Distribute the three-page set of forms. On day one, work on Step 1: Thoughts. Read the sample to the students, emphasizing that at this stage, their writing can be in short phrases or sentences.

4. On day two, have students work on Step 2: Reform Thoughts. Read the sample to them, explaining that this time their thoughts must be put into sentence form. Edit their work as they move through this stage.

5. On day three, students should fix errors in step 2. After having it checked by the teacher, they should write their completed paragraphs on the Step 3: Put Into Form sheet. Read them the sample first to show them how a paragraph should flow smoothly. With everything checked along the way, the students will only need to transfer the information from the previous page.

6. When finished, the paragraphs are ready to share!

Bag Tag

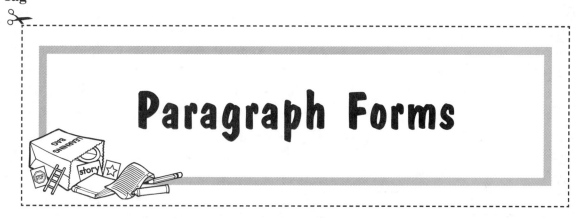

Step 1: Thoughts

Example

Topic: _____Birthday Party_____
(What are you going to write about?)

Beginning: _____age 5 birthday party_____

Fact: _____clowns came_____
(Main idea)

Detail: _____did magic tricks_____

Fact: _____cake and ice cream_____

Detail: _____chocolate cake with chocolate frosting; vanilla ice cream___

Ending: _____favorite birthday_____
(Summary)

Name: _____

Topic: _____

Beginning: _____

Fact: _____

Detail: _____

Fact: _____

Detail: _____

Ending: _____

Step 2: Reform Thoughts

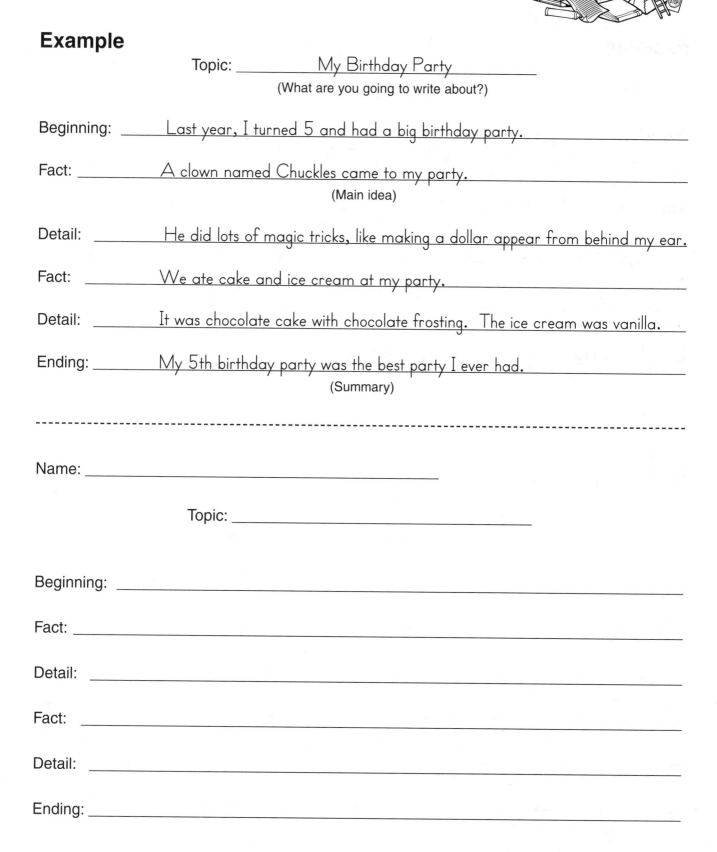

Example

Topic: _____ My Birthday Party _____
(What are you going to write about?)

Beginning: _____ Last year, I turned 5 and had a big birthday party. _____

Fact: _____ A clown named Chuckles came to my party. _____
(Main idea)

Detail: _____ He did lots of magic tricks, like making a dollar appear from behind my ear. _____

Fact: _____ We ate cake and ice cream at my party. _____

Detail: _____ It was chocolate cake with chocolate frosting. The ice cream was vanilla. _____

Ending: _____ My 5th birthday party was the best party I ever had. _____
(Summary)

- -

Name: _____

Topic: _____

Beginning: _____

Fact: _____

Detail: _____

Fact: _____

Detail: _____

Ending: _____

Step 3: Put Into Form

Example

<u>My Birthday Party</u>

     Last year, I turned 5 and had a big birthday party. A clown named Chuckles came to my party. He did lots of magic tricks, like making a dollar appear from behind my ear. We ate cake and ice cream at my party. It was chocolate cake with chocolate frosting. The ice cream was vanilla. My 5th birthday party was the best party I ever had.

- -

Name: _____

_____

_____

_____

_____

_____

_____

Pencil Roll Stories

Sequencing and organizing events are life-long writing skills. The easiest way for young students to learn how to organize their writing is to help them identify and use cue words in written text. This bag activity will help them do that.

Materials and Preparation

- ✏ 1 medium gift bag, labeled Pencil Roll Stories
- ✏ 1 copy of Pencil Rolls for each student, pages 34–35
- ✏ 2 full-length, unsharpened pencils for each student
- ✏ bits of yarn, construction paper, buttons, pipe cleaners, markers, etc. to decorate pencils
- ✏ 1 rubber band for each student

- ✏ scissors
- ✏ tape
- ✏ glue

Procedure

1. Discuss sequencing stories in terms of cue or transition words to tell that time has passed. For example, the word "first" comes at the beginning of the story. The word "next" indicates that the story has progressed, and something is happening after the beginning. "Finally" indicates something that happens at the end of a story. You may want to write a story using these words as a class.

2. It is recommended that you make a sample, complete with pencils. The pencils will become characters, who roll apart to tell the story with words and illustrations. Model how to tape on the pencils, how to glue or tape the tab of the first page under the second page, and how to roll the stories (like a scroll).

3. Hand out the Pencil Roll pages to each student. Have them write their stories, then switch with a partner to check for spelling and to make sure the stories make sense. You may also want to have an adult check their stories. It is recommended that they use lined paper first and save the Pencil Roll pages for their final drafts.

4. Once their stories have been checked, the students can cut out the stories, tape or glue the two pages together, and tape the paper to the pencils.

5. Have students decorate the pencils with the art supplies. Place a rubber band around each story to hold the pencils together. Store the rolled-up stories in the gift bag until they are ready to share.

Bag Tag ✂

Pencil Roll Stories

Pencil Rolls

Tape or glue this under the next page.

Next,

Tape this part to your pencil.

At first,

34

Pencil Rolls *(cont.)*

Tape this part to your pencil.

Finally, _____

Then, _____

Shape Poems

Writing poems can be a lot of fun, but they also require giving students structure—even if the desired outcome is non-traditional structure. Sometimes we have to "unteach." Conventional methods seem comfortable, but poems are not conventional. With that comes taking a walk through our own minds to see how it might make sense to a child.

Materials and Preparation

- ✏ 1 large gift bag, labeled Shape Poems
- ✏ 1 copy of both Teaching Posters, pages 37–38
- ✏ 1 transparency of Shape Poem Examples, page 39
- ✏ several copies of each of the Shape Poem forms, pages 40–45
- ✏ several different large pictures of things such as a frog, planet, butterfly, fish, ice-cream cone, watermelon, etc., cut out in that shape
- ✏ examples of shape poems by poets such as Jack Prelutsky (optional)

Procedure

1. Start by explaining that a shape poem is a poem written about a specific shape (star, triangle, balloon, etc.), around or inside of a drawing of that shape. Show students the Shape Poem Examples transparency so that they understand the idea. Share any other available examples of shape poems written by poets, or share any examples that you have done.

2. List the steps on Teaching Poster 1 and present an oral example of a shape poem by saying a poem aloud while moving your fingers around one of the picture shapes.

3. Using Teaching Poster 2 as a reference, stress "talking around" the shape and the use of adjectives. Have student volunteers choose a picture shape and practice "talking around" it. They will move their fingers around the shape as they speak.

4. Draw a balloon on the board. Have students brainstorm adjectives for it, then write a sample shape poem around the shape of the balloon. Explain to students that a shape poem can also have writing inside of the shape. Draw another balloon next to the original one. Write a different sample shape poem inside of the balloon. Students should understand that both ways are acceptable.

5. Explain to students that they each will write a shape poem about a shape of their choice. Show students the different shape poem forms (pages 40–45), and have them choose the shape they would like to write about. You may want to give them a blank sheet of paper as a "planning sheet" to start their poems. Have students first write a few ideas/adjectives on their planning sheet. Then have them write their shape poem. They can copy the final poem onto the shape poem form.

Bag Tag ✂

Shape Poems

Teaching Poster 1

Shape Poems

1. <u>Name</u> it! Apple

2. <u>What</u> does it do? Tastes so great

3. <u>Where</u> do you get or find it? From a tree

4. <u>Describe</u> it! Red and juicy

5. <u>Rename</u> it! Fruit

Teaching Poster 2

Shape Poems

Talk your way around the shape!

Think Adjectives!

Shape Poem Examples

Apple, Tastes so great, From a tree, Red and juicy, Fruit

Apple,
Tastes so great,
From a tree,
Red and juicy,
Fruit

Dog Shape Poem

Name _____

House Shape Poem

Name _____

Star Shape Poem

Name _____

42

Kite Shape Poem

Name _____

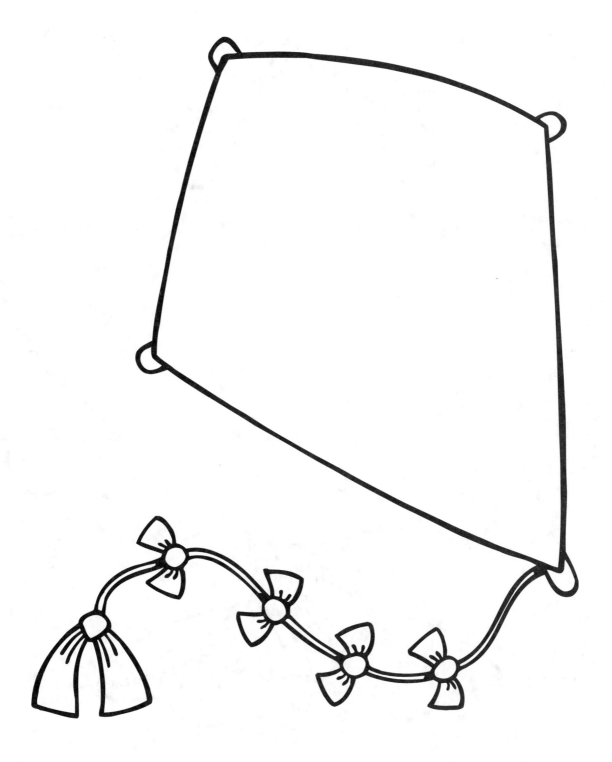

Tree Shape Poem

Name _____

Sun Shape Poem

Name _____

Sharing Bag

This bag will get passed from one student to the next throughout the year! Students will have fun filling the bag and pulling out things to share about themselves!

Materials and Preparation

✆ 2 small gift bags, each labeled My Sharing Bag (one for the boys and one for the girls)

✆ 1 copy of Body Form, pages 47–49, for each student

✆ several pieces of craft items (hair ribbons, buttons, fabric, yarn, colored paper, etc.)

✆ scissors

✆ glue

Procedure

1. This is a type of "Student of the Week" activity. Choose a different student every 1–2 weeks to be "in the spotlight." Alternate between boys and girls. For each chosen student, copy the Body Form pages (preferably on cardstock), cut them apart, and tape them together.

2. Have the chosen student take the Body Form home and complete the writing with an adult. Then, have him or her decorate the spaces around the writing by adding the craft items to represent hair, clothes, shoes, and jewelry.

3. Give the designated sharing bag to the student to fill with about six different small items from home that represent him or her. The student will present his or her Body Form and sharing bag to classmates to share about himself or herself.

4. Repeat this activity each time with a new student.

Bag Tag

Sharing Bag

Body Form

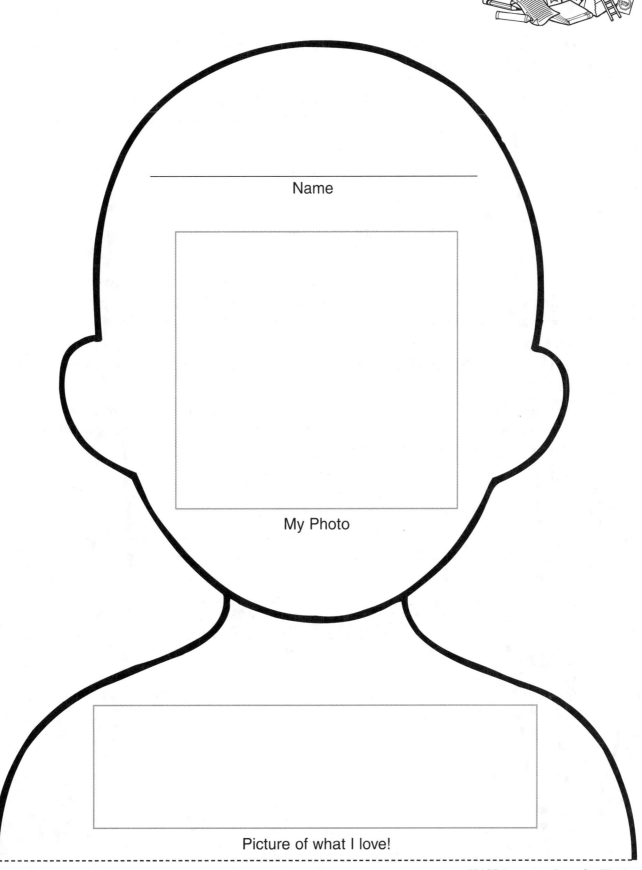

_____

Name

My Photo

Picture of what I love!

Body Form *(cont.)*

My Personal Information

I have _____ hair.

I am _____ feet, _____ inches

tall. The people in my family are _____

_____

_____ .

My favorite food is _____

_____ .

My favorite color is _____ .

I describe myself as _____ ,

_____ , and

_____ .

I love to:

_____

_____

_____

_____

I am happy when _____

I am sad when _____

48

Body Form *(cont.)*

My goals are:

_____

_____

_____

_____

_____

_____

The pets I have or want:

_____

_____

_____

_____

_____

_____

When I grow up
I want to:

_____

_____

_____

Something interesting
about me is:

_____

_____

_____

_____

Special "ME" Books

Student writing is most thoughtful and precise when coupled with confidence. This collection of books can be made throughout the year and stored in a bag for good reading. They become references so students know exactly how special each one of them is.

Materials and Preparation

- ✏ 1 large gift bag, labeled Special "ME" Books

- ✏ 1 copy of Parent Cover Letter for each student, page 51

- ✏ 1 copy of Parent Form for each student, page 52

- ✏ 1 copy of Student Book Cover for each student, page 53

- ✏ several copies of General Form, page 54. These are used by students, the teacher, and the principal for each student's book.

Procedure

1. Make and post a schedule showing what student will get recognized for each week.

2. Give the parent or set of parents a Parent Cover Letter and Parent Form along with the schedule.

3. During each student's recognized week, everyone (including classmates, parent(s), teacher, and principal) should write to that student on the forms and turn them in to you. Parents should write on the Parent Forms, and the students, teacher, and principal should write on the General Form. At the bottom of the General Form is space for anyone who wishes to draw a picture for the recognized student. If you choose, other special things could be done for that student each day of his or her week of recognition to promote confidence.

4. After collecting all the completed forms, place the Student Book Cover on top of the stack. Laminate the pages if possible, and bind the book.

5. Choose a day for sharing the book with students. Store them in the large gift bag until the end of the year. Students will treasure these keepsakes for years to come.

Bag Tag

Special "ME" Books

Parent Cover Letter

Dear Parent,

We would like to promote a feeling of confidence within each student. Your help will be appreciated to accomplish this important goal.

Each student will get a chance to have a week of recognition. We will try to do special things each day to help him or her see his or her positive attributes.

This is where you come in! There's nothing your child would like better than to hear from you. Attached, you will find a Parent Form. Please fill it out and return it without letting your son or daughter see it. It will be read and included in a book for your child to keep. Thank you for all of your support.

Sincerely,

Parent Form

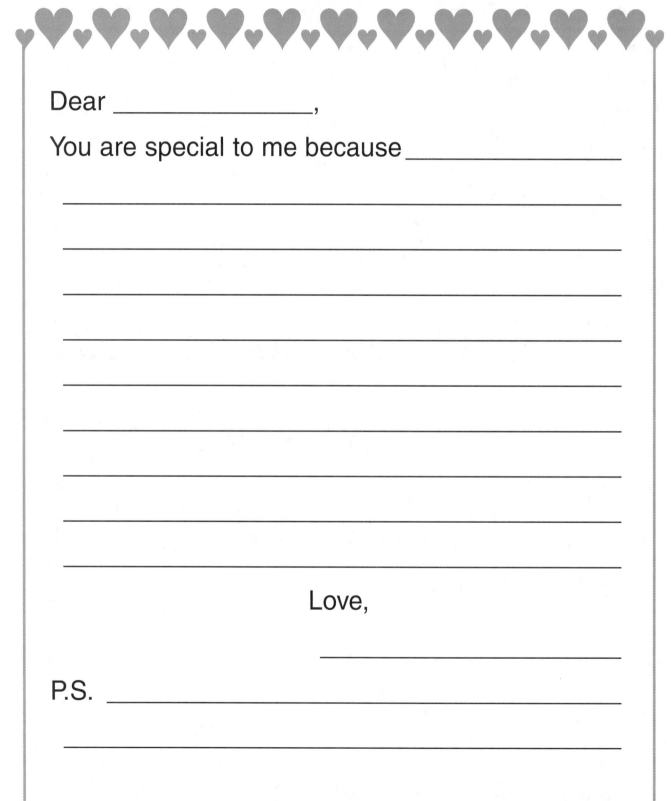

Dear _____,

You are special to me because _____

_____

_____

_____

_____

_____

_____

_____

Love,

_____

P.S. _____

_____

Student Book Cover

Name _____

You can do

what you choose . . .

because you

are you!

General Form

To: _____

You are unique because _____

_____

_____

_____

From: _____

Stop Sign Writing

When writing, many students have difficulty remembering to stop and double check that their stories include the basic story elements. This activity reminds students to stop and think about what they have already written. With time and practice, students will automatically learn to stop, check, and make revisions to their writing.

Materials and Preparation

- ✏ 1 medium gift bag, labeled Stop Sign Writing (Use to store copies and for display.)

- ✏ several copies of the Stop Sign Writing Form, page 56

- ✏ 12 feet or more of thick, red yarn (optional)

Procedure

1. Review writing stories with students, making sure to discuss the target items of the Stop Sign Writing Form.

2. Have students use the Stop Sign Writing Form for all story writing they do until it becomes natural for them to stop and think.

3. Store all blank copies of the Stop Sign Writing Form in the gift bag. Keep the bag available to students so they can easily get a new form and write stories any time.

4. Optional: Use the gift bag as a display of their writing and learning. Hook it on a hook from the ceiling, or attach it to a bulletin board with the yarn attached. As students write and complete their stories, attach them to the line of yarn until they touch the floor or fill up the space on the bulletin board. This will serve as a nice display and reminder for students to stop and think as they write.

Bag Tag

Stop Sign Writing Form

STOP
Did I
introduce my
characters?

STOP
Am I using
complete
sentences?

STOP
Am I using
description?

STOP
Does my
story have a
problem?

STOP
Is the
problem in
my story
solved?

Storyboards

Let's face it: kids love TV and movies! In this lesson, students have the opportunity to create a storyboard for their own television show. They will experience the challenge of expressing a lot in a little amount of space.

Materials and Preparation

- 1 large gift bag, labeled Storyboards
- 1 copy of Storyboard Planner per student, page 58
- 1 transparency of Storyboard Planner, page 58
- 1 large piece of chart paper
- markers, crayons, and/or colored pencils
- 1 large piece (12" x 18") of white construction paper per student (optional)

Procedure

1. Explain to the students that writers of movies and television shows use storyboards to draw and write a sketch of the show they are going to film. Tell students they will create their own storyboards for a TV show. Have them share ideas about their favorite shows, and ask them what makes them so interesting and funny. Write their ideas on the piece of chart paper and hang it in the room so the students can refer to it while they write.

2. Do an example of a storyboard on the overhead transparency, asking the students for ideas. Sketch a different picture in each box and write a sentence to go along with each one. Hand out the Storyboard Planner page to each student and have him or her sketch a storyboard of his or her own. Have each student draw a picture in each box and then write a sentence about it on the lines below. For students who are able to go a step farther, have them write dialogue bubbles in their boxes. Remind them that they do not need to use quotation marks when these characters are speaking because each character's words are contained in his or her own speech bubble.

3. When the students finish, have them trade with a partner to check for spelling and to make sure the storyboards make sense. Then have them corrected by an adult. These can be stored in the gift bag until they are ready to be shared, or used to create a final draft on larger paper.

4. If you would like the students to make a larger version, give them the large sheets of construction paper. (You may want to prepare these ahead of time by dividing each paper evenly into six squares. This can be done by dividing the short side (12") in half, and the long side (18") in thirds. Use a marker to trace over the folds so that the lines can be clearly seen.)

5. Have the students draw their final drafts in color.

6. You can choose to have the students present their storyboards to the class, or they can be hung around the room for students to look at individually.

Extension: You may choose to have the students film their shows by having them create paper figures that can move around on a backdrop. Film the students creating the shows, and invite other classes to come watch the finished products!

Bag Tag ✂

 **Storyboards**

Storyboard Planner

Name: _____ Title of Show: _____

1. _____ _____ _____	2. _____ _____ _____
3. _____ _____ _____	4. _____ _____ _____
5. _____ _____ _____	6. _____ _____ _____

Seasonal Writing

Showing a change of time or season in a story takes a lot of practice for young writers. They need to first be aware of the setting as they read library books or their reading text. One way to help students recognize time and place is to demonstrate searching for cue words. They can apply this concept to their own writing. This activity helps students to define and apply the "turn" of seasons in a concrete and visual way.

Materials and Preparation

- ✏ 1 paper lunch bag for each student
- ✏ 1 copy of Seasonal Writing Form per student, page 60
- ✏ 1 copy of Seasonal Sorting Cards per student, page 61
- ✏ colored markers
- ✏ scissors
- ✏ glue

Procedure

1. Discuss with students the "turn" of seasons as it applies to reading and writing.

2. Show examples in library books. Then have them search their own texts for examples.

3. Discuss how they knew the season that the story took place or how the season had "turned." Then discuss it in terms of cue words.

4. Give each student a copy of the Seasonal Writing Form. Show them the oval sorting spot for cue words or phrases. Then hand out the copies of Seasonal Sorting Cards and have students cut them apart. Students are to place each sorting card on the sorting spot for the season they think it belongs in. Some sorting cards can be placed in more than one season. Ask for volunteers to tell which cue words they put in each season.

5. The students should then take off the cards and keep them in order. They will write a very short story (one to two sentences per season) that shows the "turn" of seasons from one box to the next. They should include the words from the sorting cards.

6. Have students cut out the boxes from the Seasonal Writing Form out and glue them to the bottoms of each side of the bag, so that they have to "turn" it to show the next season. (Remind them to glue them in seasonal order, so that Summer doesn't come right after Winter, etc.) They can star the season in which their stories begin. Let them illustrate the season above each story part using markers. (If it is hard for them to draw on the smaller sides of the bags, have them draw pictures on paper and glue them to the bags.)

7. Finally, they should put the sorting cards inside their bags, and make a few of their own phrases for the seasons. Also have them bring in objects from home that represent each season. For example, they might bring in an orange leaf for Fall, some sand from the beach for Summer, a picture of a snowman for Winter, a flower for Spring, etc.

8. Have the students share their stories with the class, showing each of the objects they brought for the seasons. Or, you may put the bags on display in the classroom for the students to read on their own.

Seasonal Writing Form

Spring

_____

_____

_____

_____

_____

_____

_____   Sorting
                                         Spot

Summer

_____

_____

_____

_____

_____

_____   Sorting
                                         Spot

Winter

_____

_____

_____

_____

_____   Sorting
                                         Spot

Fall

_____

_____

_____

_____

_____   Sorting
                                         Spot

Seasonal Sorting Cards

blooming flowers	purple tulips	when you dive into cool water
orange and red trees	crunchy leaves	when there are blizzards
when trees begin to bud	hot sun	tasty outside barbecues
chilly air	when we pick pumpkins	icy roads
mild breezes	going to the beach	when there are boats sailing
sweater weather	frosty windows	snow and sleet

What's Next?

Students have great fun choosing topics they know their peers will enjoy finishing for them. These writings will have two different authors. They will be made to pass and share. When they compare what was written and what the original author had in mind, you will witness a very thoughtful discussion on all the possibilities.

Materials and Preparation

- ✎ 1 medium gift bag, labeled What's Next?
- ✎ 1 copy of Outside Writing Form per student, page 63
- ✎ 1 copy of Inside Writing Form per student, page 64

- ✎ 1 paper clip per student
- ✎ colored pencils and/or crayons
- ✎ scissors
- ✎ glue sticks

Procedure

1. Explain to students that they will be writing stories with a "mystery" partner. Each student will start a story, but an unknown classmate will finish it. Distribute both Writing Forms to students and model how to assemble the forms. Explain to students that they will first cut out each form along the large dashed box. On the Outside Writing Forms, students need to make two additional cuts along the two dashed lines leading up to the "fold line," making sure not to cut past it. Have them fold that loose flap up, then down again. Once the two forms are cut out, they are to turn the Outside Writing Form upside down and put glue all over the back of the form, without putting any glue on the loose flap. Then they are to line up and place the Outside Writing Form on top of the Inside Writing Form and press down to glue together. The two forms should be stuck together leaving only the flap to go up and down, and making the lines on the Inside Writing Form visible. Have them place a paper clip at the bottom of the flap to hold it to the form.

2. Once dried, have each student begin a story on the Outside Writing Form, reminding him or her that another student will finish it. He or she can then draw a picture on the top of the flap to go along with what he or she has written. Tell students to write their names or initials somewhere on the top of the flap. When finished, have students place their half-completed forms in the gift bag.

3. After all students have finished the beginnings of their stories, walk around the room with the gift bag and have each student select a story from the bag without looking. He or she is to read what the original author wrote and complete the story. Then the student can write his or her name or initials and draw a picture on the back of the flap to go with the story ending. Have students place the paper clip back where it was to hold the flap in place, and put the completed stories back in the gift bag.

4. Distribute the stories back to the original authors to read how their stories ended. Ask volunteers to share their stories. Have a class discussion about whether the story endings were different than what they had expected.

5. You may choose to have more advanced students work on more than one story.

Bag Tag ✂

What's Next?

Outside Writing Form

fold here

Inside Writing Form